Sirtfood Diet Cookbook for Beginners

A Complete Beginners Guide and Cookbook. Burn Fat Fast, Boost Your Skinny Gene and Activate Metabolism to Lose Weight Fast and Gain Muscle

David Cooper

Table of Contents

INTRODUCTION

The sirt diet is that the new way of burning excess body fat which will hamper the state of your health. In fact, this diet can help in losing weight with none quite experience regarding malnutrition or maybe starving.. This ultimately leads to the event of the genes which will easily follow the after-effects of fasting and exercising. Food items that are rich in polyphenols include coffee, kale, red wine, green tea, coffee. Once you consume any of the food items from this group, sirtuins are going to be released which will end in aging, mood swings, alongside enhancement of body metabolism. Any sort of diet that's rich within the consumption of sirtuins can help in triggering loss of weight with none got to expend the muscles. You'll get the prospect to realize a healthy body alongside a healthy lifestyle. This diet is predicated completely on the restriction of calorie intake that must be wiped out various phases. Calorie restriction of this type can help within the improvement of sirtuin production within the physical body. You would possibly be having thoughts about whether the diet is fit you or not, and that I am sure that this book goes to clear all of your doubts. You ought to confine mind that each one the food items that are included within the diet plan are very healthy. The diet are going to be providing you with the specified amount of minerals, nutrients, and vitamins. The difference of the body to the present diet will improve with time as you'll keep it up following the diet. So, the diet might end in being a touch complex for a few people to urge wont to it and follow an equivalent.

CHAPTER 1:

HOW THE SIRT DIET WORKS

The high flexibility of the Sirte diet, which according to scholars is divided into two phases, allows those who decide to follow it not to be severe in doing it, that is, the two phases of which it is characterized can be repeated even only occasionally, supporting our needs.

Phase 1 - Weight loss

Phase 1 is also known as the moment of weight loss and lasts for seven days. It is the hardest phase because they are low in calories and the diet is less varied. The first 2-3 days must not exceed 1000 kcal; therefore, the food will focus on three green or centrifuged juices accompanied by a single solid meal. From the third day onwards, the calories can increase to 1500 kcal, feeding with two green juices (or centrifuged) together with two solid meals. It is the "supersonic" phase precisely because slimming is clearly evident in this week.

Phase 2 - Maintenance

Phase 2 lasts about two weeks and is used to maintain and maintain weight loss. Nutritionists recommend three solid meals, to choose from the aforementioned Sirte foods + a green maintenance juice. The calories not to be exceeded reach 2000 kcal, but in this phase more sari is granted with glasses of wine and vegetables at will.

Exercise during phase 1

During phase 1, caloric intake is restricted ad set to 1,000. During this week and in this week only, you may decide to avoid exercise if you don't feel to. It' up to you. If you are already used to training, you may want to keep going, maybe with less intensity. If you never trained before, the suggestion is to listen to your body. Always remember that there's no need to climb a mountain during phase 1, a brisk walk will be ok and this should be sustainable for everyone.

Exercise during phase 2

During phase 2 you will gradually return to a normal calorie intake and you should feel a lot more energized so, why not put the excess energy to
good use?

Plenty of athletes from have tried this diet, so you can easily conclude that it works perfectly fine with training and workout. In order to maximize the fat- burning effect, workout while dieting is important, but it is up to you how intense you want to train.

The Advantages Of Sirtfoods Diet

There is growing evidence that sirtuin activators can have a good range of health benefits, additionally to putting together muscle and suppressing appetite. These include improving memory, helping the body to raised control blood glucose levels, and cleaning up damage from radical molecules which will build up in cells and cause cancer and other diseases. There is substantial observational evidence of the beneficial effects of taking food and drinks rich in sirtuin activators to scale back the danger of chronic disease. Sirtfood diet is especially suitable as an anti-aging regimen. Although sirtuin activators are present throughout the Plantae, only certain sorts of fruit and vegetables are large enough to be considered Sirtuin foods. Examples include tea, chocolate, Indian spice turmeric, cabbage, onion, and parsley. Many of the fruit and vegetables displayed in supermarkets, like tomatoes, avocados, bananas, lettuces, kiwis, carrots, and cucumbers, are quite scarce in sirtuin activators. However, that doesn't mean it's not worth eating, as they supply many other benefits. The beauty of a diet rich in sirt-based foods is that it's far more flexible than other diets. You'll simply eat healthily by adding some small amounts, otherwise you may have them concentrate by adding sirtfoods, and the diet could leave more calories on low-calorie days.

A notable discovery from a sirtfood diet study is that participants lost considerable weight without losing muscle. It had been common for participants to extend muscle mass, resulting in a more defined and toned appearance. This is often the sweetness of sirtfoods; they activate fat burning but also promote muscle growth, maintenance, and repair. This is often in complete contrast to other diets where weight loss generally results from both

What Is The Skinny Gene ?

Almost 95% of individuals during this world of today aren't satisfied with the sort of body or the body shape that they possess. The dimensions of the body is taken into account to be unattractive or unappealing by the bulk of the individuals. All of this ultimately leads to the event of feeling disturbed regarding the varied ways during which the form of the body are often controlled, contoured, and altered. You want to have met someone in your life who is unable to realize some bodyweight despite the sort and amount of food that they consume. Various studies and research are conducted to work out how some people don't have the tendency to realize any excess pounds while taking under consideration the habits of eating in contrast to all or any those people that seems to realize excessive weight with anything they consume. The right account this will actually be found in their genes. Nobody can ever find a gene that's perfect altogether possible aspects. While talking about the gain of weight and obesity, genetics is one such factor that we frequently fail to note. Genetics can actually play a really important role in weight gain, alongside obesity.

There are certain people that accompany the advantage of the thin genes. Such people can activate the thin genes whenever they desire while people cannot. Even once you belong to the not so lucky group, you'll choose certain things which will help in activating the genes that you simply desire. It's actually the way during which the genes interact with the encompassing environment. The thin genes or sirtuins add a lively way for altering the definite path by which the body cells function. Sirtuins are the foremost effective genes when it involves burning down body fat. This group of genes is taken into account to be special as they will activate the survival mode for the cells of the body.

All of those things are administered via a process named autophagy. Autophagy is additionally considered important for discarding waste materials from the body cells additionally to the varied sorts of unwanted particles that tend to urge stored up within the course of your time. When unwanted particles tend to urge accumulated within the cells, it can cause inflammation. The general result that's associated with the method of

restoration is of alarming nature. It can help in making the body cells look healthier and younger, and may also help in handling inflammation. The activation of the thin genes is that the primary key which will help within the process of weight loss. Not only that, but it also can help in preventing the body from health problems with various types.

Nutrition for activating the required Genes

It has been found that the character of food that folks consume, alongside the character of the environment during which they live, can show certain adverse effects on the makeup of the genes. The thin gene, also referred to as the sirtuins, are often found altogether folks. All that we'd like to try to be to seek out them out and just activate them. Some groups of individuals might get exposed to certain things counting on the genetic makeup in accordance with their weight, alongside another factors. It's possible to beat the genes if it's the most reason behind the increasing weight of the body. If administered within the proper way, a person can lose their bodyweight that's resulting in problems of several kinds.

But, there's no definite reason behind putting all the blame on the makeup of the genes for developing obesity. As already discussed before, the genes play a few 15 – 20% role in increasing weight. The remainder depends on various environmental factors. It's needed to form certain adjustments altogether those places wherever it's necessary without barely blaming the genetic makeup for being overweight. One among the foremost definite ways of doing so is by following the sirtfood diet can readily help in losing a substantial amount of weight. It'll not have any sort of adverse effects on your muscle mass also. All that you simply will got to do is to incorporate certain food items in your daily diet.

CHAPTER 2:

BASIC SIRTFOOD INGREDIENTS

There are various foods that can be included in your plan of Sirtfood Diet. This chapter is all about the various types of sirtfoods that you should include in the diet for getting the best results. The following twenty foods contain the highest amounts of sirtuin-activating polyphenols. The levels of polyphenol are not uniformly distributed in all these foods, and some of them contain higher amounts. Moreover, different types of polyphenols are present in each of them, and they are associated with special effects on the sirtuin gene.

This is why one of the most important aspects of the Sirtfood Diet is to use a variety of foods.

Each of these foods has their own impressive health qualities, but nothing compares to when they are combined.

Buckwheat

Flour that is made from buckwheat helps a lot in losing weight. The overall fat content of buckwheat is very low. In fact, the calorie count is less from normal rice or wheat. As the flour comes with a low amount of saturated form of fat, it can stop you from binge-eating or eating unnecessarily. So, it can help in facilitating and maintaining quick digestion.

Because of the low amount of fat along with a greater quantity of minerals, it can facilitate controlling diabetes of type II.

Arugula

Arugula is a great sirtfood vegetable and is low in calories. It will not only help you to lose weight but also comes with several healthy properties. Arugula is rich in chlorophyll that can help in preventing DNA and liver damage resulting from aflatoxins. For getting the best from the arugula, it is always recommended to consume this vegetable raw.It is made of 95% water, and thus it can also act as a cooling and hydrating food for the summer days. Vitamin K plays an important role in maintaining bone health.

Capers

Caper is the unripe flower bud of Capparis spinosa. It is rich in compounds of flavonoid that also includes quercetin and rutin, great sources of antioxidants.

Antioxidants can act readily in preventing free radicals that can lead to skin diseases and also cancer. Capers can help in keeping a check on diabetes. It contains several chemicals that can keep the level of blood sugar under control.

Chilies

Consumption of chilies in your daily diet can help in burning down calories. So, adding a bit of spice to your daily diet like cayenne or bird's eye chili can help in getting rid of the extra calories and help boosting up the metabolism.

It also helps in lowering the levels of blood sugar. It has also been found that people who have the habit of consuming chili in their diet can feel full easily, and thus, it can lower your food cravings.

Celery

Celery contains very low calories and that is excellent for losing weight. It can also aid in preventing dehydration as it comes with a great amount of water and electrolytes that also helps in lowering bloating.

It comes with antiseptic properties and prevents various problems of the
kidney. Consumption of this vegetable can also help in excreting toxic elements from the body. Celery comes with great amounts of vitamin K and vitamin C, along with potassium and folate.

Cocoa

Intake of cocoa, even in its chocolate form, can help in controlling weight. Cocoa comes along with fat-burning properties and is the prime reason why most of the trainers suggest mixing cocoa in shakes before exercising.

It can help in reducing inflammation and thus can also help in proper digestion. Cocoa is rich in antioxidants like polyphenols.

Coffee

Coffee is one of the most famous beverages that can be found all over the world. Coffee comes with a very low-calorie count. Caffeine is a form of natural stimulant that is abundant in coffee.

It increases the mental functionality and alertness, making the brain alert and sharpened. Caffeine can help in improving metabolism and thus can act as a great weight loss component. But do not exceed as it can affect your sleeping patterns.

Olive Oil

Olive oil has always been popular for cooking food. Olive oil that is of the extra virgin category can help you in losing weight as it is unrefined and unprocessed. It comes with a great percentage of fatty acids of mono- saturated type that plays an important role in losing weight.

Olive oil is also rich in vitamin E that is good for the health of hair and skin. It comes with great properties of anti-inflammation as well. Olive oil helps in aiding low absorption of fat and thus makes your food healthy and tasty at the same time.

Garlic

Garlic is one of those vegetables that can be found in every kitchen. Consumption of raw garlic can help in boosting energy levels that can aid in losing weight. Garlic is well known for suppressing appetite that can help you in staying full for more amount of time. Thus, with the consumption of garlic, you will be able to prevent yourself from overeating.

A strong relationship can be found between burning fat and the consumption of garlic. Garlic helps in stimulating the process of fat burning and also helps in removing harmful toxins from the body.

Green Tea

Green tea is often regarded as the healthiest type of beverage that can be found on this planet. This is mainly because green tea is full of antioxidants, along with several other plant compounds that can provide you with several health benefits like theine. Theine effect is similar to caffeine and acts as a stimulant for burning fat.

It can also help in boosting your levels of energy at the time of exercising. Green tea comes with a high concentration of minerals and vitamins, along with low content of calories. It can help in improving the metabolic rate as well.

Kale

Kale is a very popular vegetable that comes with excellent weight loss properties. It is a vegetable that is rich in antioxidants like vitamin C that performs various important functions in the body cells, along with improving the bone structure of the body.

It is rich in vitamin K and comes with excellent capabilities of binding calcium. Kale can provide you with 2.4 g of dietary fiber and thus can help in reducing the feeling of hunger. It comes with compounds rich in sulfur and can help in detoxifying the liver.

Medjool Dates

Dates are rich in dietary fibers along with fatty acids that can help in losing the extra kilos when consumed in moderation as they are very caloric. They help staying healthy and fit thanks to their protein content. Moderate consumption of dates daily can help in boosting the functioning of the immune system.

Parsley

Parsley is a very common herb that can be found in every kitchen. The leaves are rich in important compounds such as vitamin A, vitamin B, vitamin C, and vitamin K. Important minerals such as potassium and iron can also be found in parsley. As it acts as a natural form of diuretic, it can help in flushing out toxins along with any excess fluid.

Parsley is rich in chlorophyll, and it can effectively aid in losing weight. It also helps in keeping the levels of blood sugar under control. Parsley comes with certain enzymes that can help in improving the process of digestion and also helps in weight loss.

Red Endive

Endives are rich in fiber with a low-calorie count. They are rich in fiber that can help in slowing down the process of digestion and keeps the level of energy stable, a great combination of elements that can help in promoting weight loss.

Thanks to their water and fiber content, you will be able to consume more volume of food without the risk of consuming extra calories. It is rich in potassium and folate as well, important for the proper health of the heart. Potassium can act very well in lowering the level of blood pressure.

Red Onion

Red onion is rich in an antioxidant named quercetin. Red onions can help inadding extra flavor to your food without piling up extra calories. Quercetin helps in promoting burning down extra calories. It can also help in dealing with inflammation.

Red onion is rich in fiber and thus can make you feel full for a long period without the urge to consume extra calories. It can also help in improving the level of blood sugar and can deal with diabetes of type II.

Soy

It has been found that increasing the consumption of soy can help in reducing your body weight thanks to its essential amino-acids. It is rich in fiber that can help you to stay full for long.

Soy can also help in regulating the level of blood sugar and can have great control over the appetite. It can also promote better quality skin, hair, and nails, besides its weight loss benefits.

Red Wine

According to some recent studies, it has been found that drinking red wine in moderation can help in cutting down extra pounds. Red wine consists of a polyphenol named resveratrol that can aid in losing weight. This polyphenol can help in converting white fat, the larger cells that store up energy, into brown fat that can deal with obesity. It can also reduce the risk of heart attack. In fact, serious problems like Alzheimer's disease and dementia can also be reduced by consuming two glasses of red wine daily. Red wine can also prevent the development of type II diabetes.

Strawberries

Strawberries are filled with fiber, vitamins, polyphenols, zero cholesterol, and zero fat. They are also a great source of magnesium. Potassium and vitamin

C. The high fiber content also assists in losing weight.

It can help you in staying full that will reduce the chances of overeating or

snacking. A hundred grams of strawberries comes with 33 calories only. Strawberries also help in improving the system of digestion and can also readily eliminate toxins from the body.

Turmeric

Turmeric is one of the primary spices in every household. It comes with an essential antioxidant called curcumin. It helps in dealing with obesity, disorders related to the stomach, and other health problems. It can help in reducing inflammation that is linked with obesity.

Remember to add some pepper when using turmeric: the absorption of curcumin will be higher.

Walnuts

Walnuts are rich in healthy fats along with fiber that can aid in losing weight. They can provide you with a great deal of energy as well.

They contain high quantities of PUFAs or polyunsaturated fats that can help in keeping the level of cholesterol under check while alpha-linolenic acid helps in burning body fat quickly and promotes proper heart health.

CHAPTER 3:

GETTING STARTED ON SIRTFOODS

S tarting the sirtfood diet is very easy. It just takes a bit of preparation. If you do not know what kale is, or where you would find green tea, then you may have a learning curve, albeit very small. There is little in the way of starting the sirtfood diet.

Since you will be preparing and cooking healthy foods, you may want to do a few things the week you start:

1. Clear your cabinets and refrigerator of foods that are obviously unhealthy, and that might tempt you. You also will have a very low-calorie intake at the start, and you do not want to be tempted into a quick fix that may set you back. Even though you will have new recipes, you may feel that your old comfort foods are easier at the moment.

2. Go shopping for all of the ingredients that you will need for the week. If you buy what you will need, it is more cost-effective. Also, once you see the recipes, you will notice that there are many ingredients that overlap. You will get to know your portions as you proceed with the diet, but at least you will have what you need and save yourself some trips to the store.

3. Wash, dry, cut and store all of the foods that you need that way you have them conveniently prepared when you need them. This will make a new diet seem less tedious.

One necessary kitchen tool that you will need aside from the actual foods is a juicer. You will need a juicer as soon as you start the sirtfood diet. Juicers are everywhere, so they are quite easy to find, but the quality ranges greatly, however. This is where price, function, and convenience come into play. You could go to a popular department store, or you can find them online. Once you know what you are going after, you can shop around.

Here are some other tips to help you get started:

Drink your juices as the earlier meals in the day if it helps you. It is a great way to start your day for three reasons.

• It will give you energy for breakfast and for lunch, especially. By not having to digest heavy foods, your body saves time and energy usually spent on moving things around to go through all the laborious motions. You will be guaranteed to feel lighter and more energetic this way. You can always change this pattern after the maintenance phase, but you may find that you want to keep that schedule.

• Having fruits and vegetables before starchy or cooked meals, no matter how healthy the ingredients are the best way to go for your digestion. Fruits and vegetables digest more rapidly, and the breakdown into the compounds that we can use more readily. Think of it as having your salad before your dinner. It works in the same way. The heavier foods, grains, oils, meats, etc., take more time to digest. If you eat these first, they will slow things down, and that is where you have a backup of food needing to be broken down. This is also when you may find yourself with indigestion.

• Juices, especially green juices, contain phytochemicals that not only serve as anti-oxidants, but they contribute to our energy and mood. You will notice that you feel much differently after drinking a green juice than you would if you had eggs and sausage. You may want to make a food diary and note things such as this!

Be prepared to adjust to having lighter breakfasts for a little while. Most often, we fill up with high protein, carbohydrate, and high-calorie meals early in the day. We may feel that we did not get enough to eat and that we are not full at first. Oddly as it sounds, we may even miss the action of chewing. Some people need to chew their food to feel like they have had a filling meal. It is something automatic that we do not think of. Some also will miss that crunch such as with toast. Just pay attention to this, and know this is normal,

that it will pass.

CHAPTER 4:

BASIC SIRTFOOD MEAL PLAN

Week 1

Monday

Breakfast: Sirtfood Green Juice *Snack:* 2 squares of dark chocolate *Lunch:* Sirtfood Green Juice *Snack:* Sirtfood Green Juice

Dinner: Sweet Potato and Salmon Patties and Raw Artichoke Salad

Tuesday

Breakfast: Sirtfood Green Juice *Snack:* 2 squares of dark chocolate *Lunch:* Sirtfood Green Juice *Snack:* Sirtfood Green Juice

Dinner: Lemon Paprika Chicken with Vegetables

Wednesday

Breakfast: Sirtfood Green Juice *Snack:* 2 squares of dark chocolate *Lunch:* Sirtfood Green Juice *Snack:* Sirtfood Green Juice

Dinner: Tomato Soup with Meatballs

Thursday

Breakfast: Sirtfood Green Juice

Snack: Sirtfood Green Juice

Lunch: Chicken with Kale and Chili Salsa

Snack: 2 squares of dark chocolate

Dinner: Seared Tuna in Soy Sauce and Black Pepper

Friday

Breakfast: Sirtfood Green Juice *Snack:* Sirtfood Green Juice *Lunch:* Sirt Salmon Salad

Snack: 2 squares of dark chocolate

Dinner: Green Veggies Curry

Saturday

Breakfast: Sirtfood Green Juice *Snack:* Sirtfood Green Juice *Lunch:* Shrimp Tomato Stew *Snack:* 2 squares of dark chocolate

Dinner: Turkey Breast with Peppers

Sunday

Breakfast: Sirtfood Green Juice

Snack: Sirtfood Green Juice

Lunch: Goat Cheese Salad with Cranberries and Walnut

Snack: 2 squares of dark chocolate

Dinner: Spicy Chicken Stew

Week 2

Monday

Breakfast: Fluffy Blueberry Pancakes

Snack: Sirtfood Green Juice

Lunch: Caprese Skewers

Snack: 2 squares of dark chocolate

Dinner: Baked Salmon with Stir Fried Vegetables

Tuesday

Breakfast: Kale and Mushroom Frittata *Snack:* 2 squares of dark chocolate *Lunch:* Trout with Roasted Vegetables *Snack:* Banana Strawberry Smoothie *Dinner:* Mince Stuffed Peppers

Wednesday

Breakfast: Vanilla Parfait with Berries

Snack: Sirtfood Green Juice

Lunch: Arugula Salad with Turkey and Italian Dressing

Snack: 2 squares of dark chocolate

Dinner: Creamy Mushroom Soup with Chicken

Thursday

Breakfast: Super Easy Scrambled Eggs and Cherry Tomatoes

Snack: Sirtfood Green Juice

Lunch: Lemon Ginger Shrimp Salad

Snack: Blueberry Smoothie

Dinner: Lemon Chicken Skewers with Peppers

Friday

Breakfast: Overnight Oats with Strawberries and Chocolate

Snack: Sirtfood Green Juice

Lunch: Spicy Salmon with Turmeric and Lentils

Snack: 2 squares of dark chocolate

Dinner: Chicken and Broccoli Creamy Casserole

Saturday

Breakfast: Sautéed Mushrooms and Poached Eggs

Snack: Sirtfood Green Juice

Lunch: Asian Beef Salad

Snack: 2 squares of dark chocolate

Dinner: Creamy Turkey and Asparagus

Sunday

Breakfast: Banana Vanilla Pancake *Snack:* Sirtfood Green Juice *Lunch:* Shredded Chicken Bowl

Snack: 2 squares of dark chocolate

Dinner: Indian Vegetarian Meatballs

Week 3

Monday

Breakfast: Blueberry and Walnut Bake

Snack: Sirtfood Green Juice *Lunch:* Shrimp Tomato Stew *Snack:* Buckwheat Granola *Dinner:* Turkey Bacon Fajitas

Tuesday

Breakfast: Brussels Sprouts Egg Skillet

Snack: Sirtfood Green Juice

Lunch: Orange Cumin Sirloin and Simple Arugula Salad

Snack: 2 squares of dark chocolate

Dinner: Garlic Salmon with Brussel Sprouts and Rice

Wednesday

Breakfast: Banana Vanilla Pancake

Snack: Sirtfood Green Juice

Lunch: Indian Vegetarian Meatballs

Snack: Blueberry Smoothie

Dinner: Sesame Glazed Chicken with Ginger and Chili Stir-Fried Greens

Thursday

Breakfast: Super Easy Scrambled Eggs and Cherry Tomatoes

Snack: Sirtfood Green Juice

Lunch: Brussels Sprouts and Ricotta Salad

Snack: 2 squares of dark chocolate

Dinner: Sesame Tuna with Artichoke Hearts

Friday

Breakfast: Fluffy Blueberry Pancakes

Snack: Sirtfood Green Juice

Lunch: Baked Salmon with Stir Fried Vegetables

Snack: Chocolate Mousse

Dinner: Spicy Stew with Potatoes and Spinach

Saturday

Breakfast: Sautéed Mushrooms and Poached Eggs

Snack: Sirtfood Green Juice

Lunch: Roasted Butternut and Chickpeas Salad

Snack: 2 squares of dark chocolate

Dinner: Eggplant Pizza Towers

Sunday

Breakfast: Vanilla Parfait with Berries

Snack: Sirtfood Green Juice

Lunch: Arugula Salad with Turkey and Italian Dressing

Snack: Mango Mousse with Chocolate Chips

Dinner: Greek Frittata with Garlic Grilled Eggplant

Week 4

Monday

Breakfast: Brussels Sprouts Egg Skillet

Snack: Chocolate Mousse

Lunch: Creamy Turkey and Asparagus

Snack: Sirtfood Green Juice

Dinner: Spicy Indian Dahl with Basmati Rice

Tuesday

Breakfast: Vanilla Parfait with Berries

Snack: Sirtfood Green Juice *Lunch:* Lemony Chicken Burgers *Snack:* Walnut Energy Bar

Dinner: Sesame Tuna with Artichoke Hearts and Baked Sweet Potato

Wednesday

Breakfast: Blueberry and Walnut Bake *Snack:* Mango Mousse with Chocolate Chips *Lunch:* Shredded Chicken Bowl

Snack: Sirtfood Green Juice

Dinner: Creamy Broccoli and Potato Soup

Thursday

Breakfast: Chickpea Fritters

Snack: Sirtfood Green Juice

Lunch: Lemon Tuna Steaks with Baby Potatoes

Snack: Chocolate Mousse

Dinner: Sesame Tuna with Artichoke Hearts

Friday

Breakfast: Fluffy Blueberry Pancakes

Snack: Sirtfood Green Juice

Lunch: Baked Salmon with Stir Fried Vegetables

Snack: Chocolate Mousse

Dinner: Lamb, Butternut Squash and Date Tagine

Saturday

Breakfast: Overnight Oats with Strawberries and Chocolate

Snack: Sirtfood Green Juice

Lunch: Chicken and Broccoli Creamy Casserole and Baked Sweet Potato

Snack: Buckwheat Granola and ½ cup plain yoghurt

Dinner: Spinach Quiche

Sunday

Breakfast: Banana Vanilla Pancake

Snack: Sirtfood Green Juice

Lunch: Brussels Sprouts and Ricotta Salad

Snack: Energy Cocoa Balls

Dinner: Mexican Chicken Casserole

CHAPTER 5:

BREAKFAST RECIPES

1.   Honey Skyr with Nuts

Ingredients:

400 g skyr

1 tbsp. nectar (on the other hand maple syrup)

1 tsp. vanilla powder

1 bunch pecan parts (25 g)

1 bunch almond parts (25 g; unpeeled)

2 tsp. linseed oil

Planning Steps

Mix Skier with nectar and vanilla. Generally, hack pecans and almonds.

Divide the Skier into two dishes, pour the nuts over it, and shower with 1 teaspoon of linseed oil. Serve and appreciate Skyr.

2.   Soy Quark with Apple, Kiwi, and Oatmeal

Ingredients:

300 g soy quark

1 apple

2 kiwi natural products

3 tbsp. flaxseed dinner

4 tbsp. succinct cereal

Arrangement Steps

Stir soy quark until smooth and appropriate in two dishes. Clean, divide, center, and cut apples into little pieces. Strip and hack the kiwi.

Put the apple and kiwi blocks on the soy curd. Serve sprinkled with flax seeds and oats.

3.　　Blueberry and Coconut Rolls

Ingredients:

150 g whole meal flour

150 g spelled flour

1½ tsp. heating powder

1 squeeze salt

50 g crude unadulterated sweetener

4 tbsp. rape oil

250 g low-fat quark

1 egg

5 tbsp. milk (3.5% fat)

120 g blueberries

4 tbsp. ground coconut

Planning Steps

Put the flour with heating powder and salt during a bowl. Include sugar and blend. Include rapeseed oil, quark, egg and 4 tablespoons of milk and utilize a hand blender to ply into a

smooth mixture.

Wash the blueberries, pat dry, and overlay in in conjunction with rock bottom coconut under the batter.

Line a preparing sheet with material paper. Structure 9 round moves with floured hands and spot them on the preparing sheet. Brush the blueberry and coconut moves with the rest of the milk and heat during a preheated stove at 200 ° C (fan broiler 180 ° C; gas: setting 3) for 12– 15 minutes.

4. Chia Pudding with Yogurt and Strawberry Puree

Fixing

200 g strawberries (new or solidified)

2 tbsp. chia seeds

350 g yogurt (3.5% fat)

1 tsp. nectar

1 squeeze Tonka bean

50 g almond bits

20 g dim chocolate (at any rate 70% cocoa)

Directions:

Put the strawberries during a pan with slightly water and cook delicately on medium warmth in around 7 minutes and crush them if essential. Meanwhile, blend the chia seeds well with yogurt and nectar and season with Tonka beans.

Roughly cleave the almonds and chocolate. But layer chia yogurt and strawberry puree in glasses and serve sprinkled with almonds and chocolate.

5. Coconut Soy Yogurt with Pineapple and Sesame

Ingredients:

300 g soy yogurt

3 tbsp. coconut milk (45 g)

200 g pineapple mash

3 tsp. sesame

3 tsp. syrup

2 tbsp. delicate oats

Directions:

Mix the soy yogurt with coconut milk. Cut the pineapple mash into pieces.

Fry the pineapple pieces during a hot dish with 1 teaspoon syrup and 1 teaspoon sesame over medium-high warmth for 4-5 minutes, letting them caramelize marginally. At that point expel the skillet from the oven and let it cool.

Fill coconut soy yogurt in two dishes, orchestrate pineapple on top, sprinkle with residual sesame and cereal, and shower with 1 teaspoon syrup.

6.   Savvy Whole meal Spelled Rolls

Ingredients:

350 g whole meal spelled flour

150 g spelled flour type 1050

1 tsp. salt

1 parcel dried yeast or 1/2 3D square of latest yeast

½ tsp. crude genuine sweetener

355 ml oat drink (oat milk)

1 tbsp. cereal

1 tsp. poppy seeds

Directions:

Mix flour with salt, include yeast and sugar and manipulate with

350 ml oat drink to a smooth and versatile batter. Leave it shrouded during a warm spot for thirty minutes to hour.

Then manipulate once more. Split the batter into two long frankfurters and gap it into five pieces. Shape the pieces into balls and spot on a preparing sheet secured with heating paper. Somewhat cut within the middle with a blade, brush with the rest of the oat drink and sprinkle with cereal and poppy seeds.

Let the mixture pieces rest during a warm spot for an extra half- hour. Preheat the broiler to 200 degrees (fan stove 180 degrees). At that point slide the sheet into the broiler and spot a flame- resistant holder with some water on rock bottom of the stove. Heat the moves for around 20 minutes until they're brilliant yellow. At that point expel from the stove and let cool.

7.   Chocolate Banana Spread

Ingredients:

50 g dull chocolate

250 g without lactose curd cheddar (20% fat)

2 tbsp. oat drink (oat milk)

1 banana

4 cuts oat bread

Directions:

Grate dull chocolate. Put around 1 tbsp. of the grate.

Mix the curd cheddar with the oat drink until smooth. Crease within the bottom chocolate.

Peel the banana and cut it at an edge.

Brush the bread with the chocolate curd, organize the banana cuts on the very best and sprinkle with the rest of the chocolate shavings.

CHAPTER 6:

SNACKS

8.   Crunchy And Chewy Granola

Preparation Time: 45 minutes

Cooking Time: 60 minutes

Servings: 20

Ingredients:

1 tbsp. flax seeds 1/4 tsp. salt

1/2 tsp. cinnamon

1/2 cup honey

2 tbsp. brown-sugar 3/4 cup rolled oats

1/2 cup almonds, slivered 1/2 cup golden raisins 1/2 cup dried cranberries

Directions:

Pre-heat oven to 300°F. Line baking tray with parchment paper.

Mix flax seeds, cinnamon, honey, sugar oats and almonds. Insert 1 cup hot water, then mix together with hands. Spread into a thin layer over the baking tray.Bake for 50-60 minutes, until gold brown. Remove from the oven and let cool.Stir in dried fruit. Put the granola in an airtight jar or tub. It will last around two weeks.

Nutrition Facts: Calories: 233 Fat: 13g Carbohydrates: 31g Protein: 5g

9.   Power Balls

Preparation Time: 15 minutes

Cooking Time: 2 minutes

Servings: 20

Ingredients:

1 cup old fashion oats

1/4 cup quinoa cooked using 3/4 cup orange juice 1/4 cup shredded unsweetened coconut

1/3 cup dried cranberry/raisin blend 1/3 cup dark chocolate chips

1/4 cup slivered almonds

1 tbsp. peanut butter

Directions:

Cook quinoa in orange juice. Bring to boil and simmer for approximately 15 minutes. Let cool. Combine quinoa and the remaining ingredients into a bowl.

With wet hands and combine ingredients and roll in ball sized chunks. Put in a container and let cool in the fridge for at least 2 hours before eating them.

Nutrition Facts:

Calories: 189 Fat: 11g Carbohydrates: 22g Protein: 5g

10. Sirt Muesli

Preparation Time: 15 minutes

Cooking Time: 0 minutes

Servings: 1

Ingredients:

½ oz. buckwheat flakes

½ oz. buckwheat puffs

½ oz. shredded coconut

2 Medjool dates, pitted and chopped 4 walnuts, chopped

1 tbsp cocoa nibs

4 oz. strawberries, hulled and chopped 4 oz. plain Greek yogurt

Directions:

Simply mix the dry ingredients and place them in an airtight container so that they are ready to eat. If you want, you can make it in bulk by multiplying the quantities.

To enjoy the sirt muesli, put the yogurt in bowl, put strawberries on top and then add the muesli.

Nutrition Facts:

Calories: 368 Fat: 16g Carbohydrates: 54g Protein: 26g

11. Sirtfood Bites

Preparation Time: 35 minutes

Cooking Time: 0 minutes

Servings: 12

Ingredients:

4 oz. walnuts

1 oz. 85% dark chocolate 8 oz. Medjool dates, pitted 1 tbsp. cocoa powder

1 tbsp. ground turmeric

1 tbsp. extra virgin olive oil

1 tsp. vanilla extract, unsweetened 2 tbsp. water

Directions:

Put the walnuts and chocolate in a food processor and process until you have an even mixture. Add all the remaining ingredients except water and combine until the mixture forms a disc. Depending on the consistency of the mixture, you may or may not have to add the water; you don't want it to be too sticky. Shape the mixture into bite-sized balls using your wet hands and roll them in cocoa powder. Refrigerate for at least 1 hour in an airtight container before eating them.

They last up to 1 week in the fridge.

Nutrition Facts:

Calories: 127kcal Fat: 6g Carbohydrates: 14g Protein: 4g

12. Dark Chocolate Pretzel Cookies

Preparation Time: 40 minutes

Cooking Time: 17 minutes

Servings: 4

Ingredients:

1 cup yogurt

1/2 tsp. baking soda 1/4 tsp salt

1/4 tsp. cinnamon

4 Tbsp. butter, softened 1/3 cup brown sugar

1 egg

1/2 tsp. vanilla

1/2 cup dark chocolate chips 1/2 cup pretzels chopped

Directions:

Pre Heat oven to 350°F.In a bowl, whisk together sugar, butter, vanilla, and egg. In another bowl, stir together the flour, baking soda, and salt.

Pour the liquid mix over the flour mix along with the chocolate chips and pretzels and stir until just blended.

Drop large spoonfuls of dough on a baking tray lined with parchment paper.

Bake for 15-17 minutes, or until the bottoms are crispy. Allow cooling on

a wire rack.

Nutrition Facts:

Calories: 290 Fat: 15g Carbohydrates: 36g Protein: 3g

13.　Pear, Cranberry And Chocolate Crisp

Preparation Time: 40 minutes

Cooking Time: 45 minutes

Servings: 8

Ingredients:

1/2 cup flour

1/2 cup brown sugar 1 tsp. cinnamon

⅛ tsp. salt

3/4 cup yogurt 1/4 cup apples

1/3 cup butter, melted 1 tsp vanilla

1 tbsp. brown sugar

1/4 cup dried cranberries 1 tsp lemon juice

1 pear, diced

2 handfuls of dark chocolate chips

Directions:

Pre-heat oven to 375°F. Spray a casserole dish with a cooking spray. Put flour, sugar, cinnamon, salt, apple, yogurt and butter into a bowl and mix. Pour it on a baking tray lined with parchment paper.

In a large bowl, combine sugar, lemon juice, vanilla, pear, and cranberries. Pour this fruit mix along with chocolate chips over the baking tray. Bake for 45 minutes. until golden. Cool before serving.

Nutrition Facts:

Calories: 239kcal Fat: 5g Carbohydrates: 46g Protein: 3g

14. Potato Bites

Preparation Time: 10 minutes

Cooking Time: 20 minutes

Servings: 3

Ingredients:

1 potato, sliced

2 bacon slices,

cooked and crumbled

1 small avocado, pitted and cubed Cooking spray

Directions:

Spread potato slices on a lined baking sheet, spray with cooking oil, introduce in the oven at 350°F, bake for 20 minutes, arrange on a platter, top each slice with avocado, and crumbled bacon and serve as a snack.

Nutrition Facts:

Calories 180 kcal, Fat 4g, Carbohydrates 8g, Protein 6g

CHAPTER 7:

MAIN DISHES

15.   Turmeric Baked Salmon

Preparation Time: 15 minutes **Cooking Time:** 30 minutes

Servings: 1

Ingredients:

6 oz. Salmon fillet, skinned 1 tsp. extra virgin olive oil 1 tsp. Ground turmeric

¼ lemon, juiced

For the sauce:

1 tsp. extra virgin olive oil

1 oz. Red onion, finely chopped 1 oz. Tinned green peas

1 Garlic clove, finely chopped

1-inch fresh ginger, finely chopped 1 Bird's eye chili, thinly sliced

4 oz. Celery cut into small cubes

1 tsp Mild curry powder 1 Tomato, chopped

½ cup vegetable stock

1 tbsp. parsley, chopped

Directions :Heat the oven to 400°F. Start cooking the sauce. Heat a skillet over a moderate --low heat, then add the olive oil then the garlic, onion, ginger, chili, celery.

Stir lightly for two --3 minutes until softened but not colored, then add the curry powder and cook for a further minute. Put in tomato, green peas and stock and simmer for 10/15 minutes depending on how thick you enjoy your sauce. Meanwhile, combine turmeric, oil and lemon juice and rub the salmon. Put on a baking tray and cook for 10 minutes in the oven. Serve the salmon with the celery sauce.

Nutrition Facts:

Calories: 360 Fat: 8g Carbs: 10g Protein: 40g

16.   Baked Potatoes With Spicy Chickpea Stew

Preparation Time: 10 minutes

Cooking Time: 60 minutes

Servings: 4

Ingredients:

4 baking potatoes, pricked around 2 tbsp. olive oil

2 red onions, finely chopped

4 tsp. garlic, crushed or grated 1-inch ginger, grated

1/2 tsp chili flakes

2 tbsp. cumin seeds 2 tbsp. turmeric Splash of water

2 tins chopped tomatoes

2 tbsp. cocoa powder, unsweetened 2 tins chickpeas – do not drain

2 yellow peppers, chopped 2 tbsp.

Directions:

Preheat the oven to 400F; and start preparing all ingredients. When the oven is ready, put in baking potatoes and cook for 50min-1 hour until they are done.

While potatoes are cooking, put olive oil and sliced red onion into a large

wide saucepan and cook lightly, using the lid, for 5 minutes until the onions are tender but not brown.

Remove the lid and add ginger, garlic, cumin and cook for a further minute on a very low heat. Then add the turmeric and a tiny dab of water and cook for a few more minutes until it becomes thicker and the consistency is ok.

Then add tomatoes, cocoa powder, peppers, chickpeas with their water and salt. Bring to the boil, and then simmer on a very low heat for 45-50 minutes until it's thick. Finally stir in the 2 tbsp. of parsley, and some pepper and salt if you desire, and also serve the stew with the potatoes.

Nutrition Facts:

Calories: 520 Fat: 8g Carbohydrate: 91g Protein: 32g

17. Kale And Red Onion Dhal With Buckwheat

Preparation Time: 5 minutes

Cooking Time: 35 minutes

Servings: 4

Ingredients:

1 tbsp. olive oil

1 small red onion, sliced

3 garlic cloves, crushed or grated 2-inch ginger, grated

1 bird's eye chili deseeded, chopped 2 tsp. turmeric

2 tsp. garam masala 6oz snow peas

2 cups coconut milk, unsweetened 1 cup water

1 cup carrot, thinly sliced 6oz buckwheat

Directions:

Place the olive oil into a large, deep skillet and then add the chopped onion. Cook on a very low heat, with the lid for 5 minutes until softened. Add the ginger, garlic and chili and cook 1 minute. Add turmeric and garam masala along with a dash of water and then cook for 1 minute. Insert the snow peas, coconut milk and 1 cup water. Mix everything together and cook for 20 minutes on low heat with the lid. Stir occasionally and add a bit more water if the dhal begins to stick.

After 20 minutes add the carrot, stir thoroughly and cook for a further 5 minutes.

While the dhal is cooking, steam the buckwheat in salted boiling water for 15 minutes, drain it and serve it with the dhal.

Nutrition Facts:

Calories: 340 Fat: 4g Carbohydrate: 30g Protein: 4g

18. Kale, Edamame And Tofu Curry

Preparation Time: 30 minutes

Cooking Time: 45 minutes

Servings: 4

Ingredients:

1 tbsp. oil - 1 big onion, chopped

4 cloves garlic, peeled and grated

1 3-inch fresh ginger, peeled and grated 1 red chili, deseeded and thinly sliced 1/2 tsp. ground turmeric

1/4 tsp. cayenne pepper 1 tsp. paprika

1/2 tsp. ground cumin 1 tsp. salt

8 oz. dried red lentils

2 oz. soya edamame beans 8 oz. firm tofu, cubed

2 tomatoes, roughly chopped

Juice of 1 lime

½ cup parsley, stalks removed

Directions:

Put the oil in a pan on medium heat. When the oil is hot, add the onion and cook 5 minutes. Add ginger, garlic and chili and cook for further 2 minutes. Add turmeric, cayenne, paprika, cumin and salt. Stir and add red lentils, soya edamame beans and tomatoes. Pour in 4 cups boiling water and then bring to a simmer for about 10 minutes, then lower the heat and cook for a further 40 minutes until the curry becomes thicker and all flavors are blended together. Add lime juice and parsley, stir and serve.

Nutrition Facts: Calories: 325 Fat: 6g Carbs: 77g Protein: 28g

19. Lemon Chicken With Spinach, Red Onion, And Salsa

Preparation Time: 30 minutes

Cooking Time: 35 minutes

Servings: 1

Ingredients:

4oz chicken breast, skinless, boneless 1 large tomato

1 chili, finely chopped

1oz capers

Juice of 1/2 lemon

2 tbsp. extra-virgin olive oil 2 cups spinach

20g red onion, chopped

2 tsp chopped garlic 3oz buckwheat

Directions:

Heat the oven to 400°F.To make the salsa, chop the tomato very finely and put it with its liquid in a bowl. The liquid is very important because it's very tasty.

Mix with chili, capers, onion, 1tbsp oil and some drops of lemon juice. Marinate the chicken breast with garlic, lemon juice and ½tbsp oil for 10 minutes.

Heat an ovenproof skillet until warm, add the chicken and cook for a minute on every side, until light gold, then move to the oven (put on a baking tray if your pan is not ovenproof) for 5 minutes until cooked.

Remove from the oven, and cover with foil. Leave to rest for 5 minutes before serving. Meanwhile, sauté the spinach for 5 minutes with ½tbsp oil and 1tbsp garlic. Serve alongside chicken with salsa and spinach.

Nutrition Facts: Calories: 342 Fat: 8g Carbs: 18g Protein: 33g

20.   Smoked Salmon Omelet

Preparation Time: 10 minutes

Cooking Time: 15 minutes

Servings: 1

Ingredients:

2 eggs

4oz Smoked salmon, chopped 1/2 tsp. Capers

½ cup Rocket, chopped 1 tsp Parsley, chopped

1 tsp extra virgin olive oil

Directions:

Crack the eggs into a bowl and whisk well. Add the salmon, capers, rocket and parsley. Heat the olive oil in a skillet.

Add the egg mixture and, with a spatula, move the mix round the pan until it's even.

Reduce the heat and allow the omelet cook. Twist the spatula around the edges to lift them, add salmon and rocket and fold the omelet in 2.

Nutrition Facts:

Calories: 303 Fat: 22g Carbohydrate: 12g Protein: 23g

21. Broccoli And Pasta

Preparation Time: 20 minutes

Cooking Time: 10 minutes

Servings: 2

Ingredients:

5 oz. spaghetti

5 oz. broccoli

1 garlic clove, finely chopped 3 tbsp. extra virgin olive oil

2 Shallots sliced

¼ tsp. crushed chilies 12 sage shredded leaves

Grated parmesan (optional)

Directions:

Put broccoli in boiling water for 5 minute, then add spaghetti and cook until both pasta and broccoli are done (around 8 to 10 minutes).

In the meantime, heat the oil in a frying pan and add shallots and garlic. Cook for 5 minutes until it becomes golden.

Mix chilies and sage to the pan and gently cook for more 1 minute. Drain pasta and broccoli; mix with the shallot mixture in the pan, add some Parmesan, if desired and serve.

Nutrition Facts:

Calories: 350 Fat: 8g Carbs: 38g Protein: 6g

22. Artichokes and Kale with Walnuts

Preparation Time: 10 minutes

Cooking Time: 30 minutes

Servings: 2

Ingredients:

1 cup of artichoke hearts 1 tbsp. parsley, chopped

½ cup of walnuts

1 cup of kale, torn

1 cup of Cheddar cheese, crumbled

½ tbsp. balsamic vinegar 1 tbsp. olive oil

Salt and black pepper, to taste

Directions:

Preheat the oven to 250°-270°Fahrenheit and roast the walnuts in the oven for 10 minutes until lightly browned and crispy and then set aside.

Add artichoke hearts, kale, oil, salt and pepper to a pot and cook for 20-25 minutes until done.

Add cheese and balsamic vinegar and stir well. Divide the vegetables in two plates and garnish with roasted walnuts and parsley.

Nutrition Facts:

Calories: 152 kcal; Fat: 32g; Carbohydrates: 59g; Protein: 23g

23.   Pecan Crusted Chicken Breast

Preparation Time: 20 minutes

Cooking Time: 35 minutes

Servings: 4

Ingredients:

½ cup whole wheat bread, dried 1/3 cup pecans

2 tbsp. Parmesan

Salt and ground pepper 1 egg white

4 chicken breasts slices, boneless and skinless (6 to 8 oz. each)

1 tbsp. grapeseed oil Lemon cuts, for serving 1 cup mixed greens 1tbsp olive oil

Directions:

Preheat oven to 425°F. In a food processor, blitz bread, pecans and Parmesan; season with salt and pepper until you get thin breadcrumbs. Move to a bowl. In another bowl, beat egg white until foamy. Season chicken with salt and pepper. Coat each chicken breast slice with egg white first, then put it in the breadcrumb bowl and mix until completely covered.

In a large nonstick ovenproof skillet heat grapeseed oil over medium heat. When hot, put in chicken breasts cook until gently seared, 1 to 3 minutes.

Turn chicken over and put the skillet in the oven. Cook until chicken is done (around 8 to 12 minutes). Serve chicken with lemon cuts and a plate of mixed greens with olive oil lemon and salt.

Nutrition Facts:

Calories: 250 Fat: 8g Carbohydrates: 27g Protein: 17g

CHAPTER 8:

SIDE DISHES

24.   Bake Kale Walnut

Preparation Time: 10 minutes **Cooking Time:** 30 minutes

Servings: 4

Ingredients

1 medium red onion, finely chopped

¼ cup extra virgin olive oil 2 cups baby kale

½ cup half-and-half cream

½ cup walnuts, coarsely chopped 1/3 cup dry breadcrumbs

½ tsp ground nutmeg Salt and pepper to taste

¼ cup dry breadcrumbs

2 tbsp. extra virgin olive oil

Directions

Preheat oven to 350 degrees F. In a skillet, sauté onion in olive oil until tender. In a large bowl, combine cooked onion, kale, cream, walnuts, breadcrumbs, nutmeg and salt and pepper to taste, mixing well. Transfer to a greased 1-1/2-qt. baking dish. Combine topping ingredients and sprinkle over the kale mixture. Bake, uncovered, for 30 minutes or until lightly browned.

Nutrition Facts: Calories: 555 Fat: 31g Carbs: 65g Protein: 26g

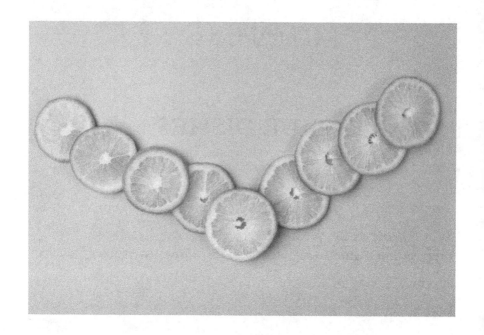

CHAPTER 9:

SAUCES AND DRESSINGS

25. Mung Sprouts Salsa

Preparation Time: 10 minutes

Cooking Time: 0 minutes

Servings: 2

Ingredients:

1 red onion, chopped

2 cups mung beans, sprouted A pinch of red chili powder

1 green chili pepper, chopped 1 tomato, chopped

1 tsp chaat masala

1 tsp lemon juice

1 tbsp. coriander, chopped

Directions:

In a salad bowl, mix onion with mung sprouts, chili pepper, tomato, chili powder, chaat masala, lemon juice, coriander and pepper, toss well, divide into small cups and serve.

Nutrition Facts:

Calories 100 kcal, Fat 2g, Carbohydrate 3g, Protein 6g

CHAPTER 10:

DINNER RECIPES

26.   Broccoli, Yellow Peppers & Beef Stir Fry

Preparation time: 5 minutes

Cooking time: 20 minutes

Servings: 2

Ingredients:

1/2 pound beef 1 cup Broccoli

1/2 cup sliced Yellow Peppers 1/2 cup chopped onions

1 Tablespoon. Sesame seeds 1 Teaspoon oil

Directions:

Marinade beef in a Super foods marinade. Stir fry drained beef in coconut oil for few minutes, add all vegetables and stir fry for 2 more minutes. Add the rest of the marinade and stir fry for a minute. Serve with brown rice or quinoa.

Nutrition:

Calories: 107 Net carbs: 10g Fat: 2.1g Fiber: 5g Protein: 10g

27. Chinese Celery, Mushrooms & Fish Stir Fry

Preparation time: 5 minutes

Cooking time: 10 minutes

Servings: 2

Ingredients:

1/2 pound fish fillets 1 cup Chinese Celery

1 cup Mushrooms sliced in half 1/2 cup peppers sliced diagonally 1 Teaspoon oil

Directions:

Marinade fish in a Super foods marinade. Stir fry drained fish in coconut oil

for few minutes, add all vegetables and stir fry for 2 more minutes. Add the rest of the marinade and stir fry for a minute. Serve with brown rice or quinoa.

Nutrition:

Calories: 24 Fat: 0.2g Protein: 5g

28.   Pork, Green Pepper and Tomato Stir Fry

Preparation time: 5 minutes

Cooking time: 20 minutes

Servings: 2

Ingredients:

1/2 pound cubed pork 1 cup Green Peppers

1/2 cup sliced Tomatoes

1 teaspoon. Ground black pepper 1 Teaspoon oil

Directions:

Marinade pork In a super foods marinade. Stir fry drained pork in coconut oil for few minutes, add all vegetables and stir fry for 2 more minutes. Add the rest of the marinade and stir fry for a minute. Serve with brown rice or quinoa.

Nutrition:

Calories: 86 Net carbs: 2.7g Fat: 2.7g Fiber: 1.9g Protein: 11.6g

29.   Pork, Red & Green Peppers, Onion & Carrots Stir Fry

Preparation time: 5 minutes

Cooking time: 20 minutes

Servings: 2

Ingredients:

1/2 pound cubed pork

1/2 cup chopped Red Peppers 1/2 cup chopped Green Peppers 1/2 cup sliced onion

1/2 cup sliced carrots 1 Teaspoon oil

Directions:

Marinade pork in a super foods marinade. Stir fry drained pork in coconut oil for few minutes, add all vegetables and stir fry for 2 more minutes. Add the rest of the marinade and stir fry for a minute. Serve with brown rice or quinoa.

Nutrition:

Calories: 118 Net carbs: 0.7g Fat: 2.6g Fiber: 1g Protein: 22.3g

30.   Chicken Edamame Stir Fry

Preparation time: 5 minutes

Cooking time: 15 minutes

Servings: 2

Ingredients:

1/2 pound chicken

1 cup Edamame pre-cooked in boiling water for 3 minutes 1/2 cup sliced carrots

1 Teaspoon oil

Directions:

Marinade chicken in a super foods marinade. Stir fry drained chicken in coconut oil for few minutes, add all vegetables and stir fry for 2 more minutes. Add the rest of the marinade and stir fry for a minute. Serve with brown rice or quinoa.

Nutrition:

Calories: 295 Net carbs: 12.3g Fat: 13.1g Protein: 31.6g

31. Chicken, Zucchini, Carrots and Baby Corn Stir Fry

Preparation time: 5 minutes

Cooking time: 15 minutes

Servings: 2

Ingredients:

1/2 pound chicken 1 cup Zucchini

1/2 cup sliced Carrots 1/2 cup Baby Corn

1 Tablespoon. Chopped Cilantro 1 Teaspoon oil

Directions:

Marinade chicken in a super foods marinade. Stir fry drained chicken in coconut oil for few minutes, add all vegetables and stir fry for 2 more minutes. Add the rest of the marinade and stir fry for a minute. Serve with brown rice or quinoa over bed of lettuce.

Nutrition:

Calories: 187 Net carbs: 7.4g Fat: 6g Fiber: 5.7g Protein: 26.2g

CHAPTER 11:

SOUPS

32.   Mushroom and Tofu Soup

Ingredients:

Two oz. dried porcini mushroom

One pound button mushroom

Half pound fresh shitake mushroom

Two tbsps. Of each

Soy sauce

Salt

One head of fresh garlic (halved)

Six ginger slices (fresh)

12 oz. firm or soft tofu (cubed)

One cup fresh cilantro (chopped)

Three tbsps. Fresh chives (chopped)

Method:

Add two cups of lukewarm water to a bowl and add dried mushrooms thereto. Let it sit for half-hour. If the mushrooms are sandy, you'll got to agitate an equivalent occasionally.Line a kitchen strainer with cheesecloth. Take a bowl and place it under the strainer to store all the liquid. Drain the soaked mushroom through the strainer and twist the cheesecloth for getting all the juice.

Pull out the stems of the shitake mushrooms and slice the caps.

Add water consistent with your required quantity of the soup to the mushroom broth.

Take a pot and add all the mushrooms thereto alongside the broth. Add salt, ginger, and garlic thereto. Bring it to a boil.

Reduce the warmth and simmer the soup for half-hour.

Remove the mushrooms, garlic, and ginger from the soup and add soy thereto.

Bring the soup to a boil and add cubes of tofu thereto.

Add sliced shitake mushroom caps to the soup and simmer it for 10 minutes.

Add cilantro and chives from the highest and provides it a stir.

Check the seasoning and serve hot.

33. Chestnut Soup with Pear and Nut Topping

Ingredients:

1 shallot

4 parsnips

400 g chestnuts (pre-cooked; vacuumed)

2 tbsp. oil

600 ml vegetable stock

30 g hazelnut bits (2 tbsp.)

1 pear

1 tsp. nectar

½ tsp. turmeric powder

2 tbsp. squeezed orange

200 g topping

Salt

Pepper

2 stems parsley

Directions:

Peel the shallot, clean, strip, and wash the parsnips. Cleave the shallot and 1 parsnip. Generally cut chestnuts.

Heat 1 tablespoon of oil during a pot. Braise shallot in it over medium warmth for 2 minutes, include chestnuts and parsnip pieces and braise for 3 minutes. Pour within the stock and cook over medium warmth for around quarter-hour.

Meanwhile, dice the rest of the parsnips. Cleave hazelnuts. Wash, quarter, center, and cut the pear into blocks.Heat the rest of the oil during a glance for gold garnish. Fry the parsnip 3D shapes for 5-7 minutes. At that point include nuts, pears, nectar, turmeric, and squeezed orange and caramelize for 2 minutes over medium warmth. Puree the soup with cream and season with salt and pepper. Wash parsley, shake dry and cleave. Pour the fixing over the soup and sprinkle with parsley.

34.   Kale and Toasted Walnut Soup.
Ingredients

two tsp extra virgin olive oil

30g red onion, sliced

30g celery, sliced

One garlic clove, sliced

one tsp dried thyme

75g preserved or preserved white beans, such as cannellini or haricot

500ml vegetable stock

50g kale, usually chopped

Four pecan halves, chopped

Method

throughout a medium saucepan, heat one teaspoon of the olive oil over a low–medium heat and fry the red onion, celery and garlic for 2–3 minutes. At the aim once they have 5, add the thyme, beans and stock and bring to embrace bubble.Simmer for twenty five thirty over low heat, then add the kale and cook for a further ten 5. When all the vegetables square measure square measure sauteed, combine. You might have to add barely barely barely is too thick. On the off likelihood that it looks flavorsome watery before you combine it, basically increase the heat and leave it cajan pea bubble 5 it's thicker.whereas the soup is cooking, heat your stove to 160°C/gas three and toast your walnuts for 10–15 5 so as that they are pleasantly browned – watch them carefully as they will without doubt without doubt without doubt without doubt to consumed.Serve your soup showered with the remaining teaspoon two oil oil with oil pecans

CHAPTER 12:

SALADS

35.   Sprouts And Apples Snack Salad

Preparation Time: 10 minutes

Cooking Time: 0 minutes

Servings: 4

Ingredients: 1 lb. Brussels sprouts, shredded 1 cup walnuts, chopped

1 apple, cored and cubed

1 red onion, chopped 3 tbsp. red vinegar

1 tbsp. mustard - ½ cup olive oil

1 garlic clove, crushed Black pepper to the taste

Directions:

In a salad bowl, mix sprouts with apple, onion and walnuts. In another bowl, mix vinegar with mustard, oil, garlic and pepper, whisk really well, add this to your salad, toss well and serve as a snack.

Nutrition Facts:

Calories 120 kcal, Fat 2g, Carbohydrate 8g, Protein 6g

36. Moroccan Leeks Snack Salad

Preparation Time: 10 minutes

Cooking Time: 0 minutes

Servings: 4

Ingredients:

1 bunch radishes, sliced 3 cups leeks, chopped

1 and ½ cups olives, pitted and sliced

A pinch of turmeric powder 1 cup cilantro, chopped Salt to taste

Black pepper to taste 2 tbsp. olive oil

Directions:

In a bowl, mix radishes with leeks, olives and cilantro. Add black pepper, oil and turmeric, toss to coat and serve.

Nutrition Facts:

Calories 135kcal, Fat 1g, Carbohydrate18g, Protein 9g

CHAPTER 13:

VEGETARIAN RECIPES

37. Sweet Potatoes with Asparagus, Eggplant and Halloumi
Ingredients:

1 aborigine

9 tbsp oil bean stew drops

Salt

Pepper

2 yams

1 red bean stew pepper

2 tbsp sunflower seeds

1 bundle green asparagus

4 tbsp juice

200 g chickpeas (can; trickle weight)

½ group basil

½ group lemon demulcent

1 tsp mustard

½ tsp turmeric powder

1 tsp nectar

300 g halloumi

Planning Steps

Clean, wash and cut the eggplant. Warmth 2 tablespoons of oil during a dish and sauté the aborigine cuts in medium warmth on the two sides for 5–7 minutes until brilliant earthy colored and

season with bean stew drops, salt, and pepper. Expel from the skillet and put it during a secure spot. Within the interim, strip the yam and cut it into 3D squares. Split the stew lengthways, expel the stones, wash and dig cuts. Warmth 1 tablespoon of oil within the dish, fry the yam 3D squares in it for 10 minutes. Include 1 tbsp sunflower seeds and stew cuts and season with salt and pepper. Wash asparagus as an afterthought, remove the woody closures, and strip the lower third of the stalks if essential. Warmth 1 tablespoon of oil within the skillet, fry the asparagus in it for five minutes over medium warmth. Deglaze with 1 tablespoon of juice, pour in 2 tablespoons of water and spread and cook for an extra 3 minutes. Rinse the chickpeas and permit them to channel. Wash the basil and lemon emollient, shake dry and slash. Blend chickpeas in with half the herbs and 1 tablespoon of oil and season with salt and pepper. Whisk the rest of the oil with the remainder of juice, mustard, turmeric and nectar, season with salt and pepper, and blend within the rest of the herbs.

Cut the halloumi and cut during a hot container on the two sides for five minutes over medium warmth until brilliant yellow.

Arrange yams, aubergine cuts on plates, present with chickpeas, asparagus, and halloumi and shower with the dressing. Sprinkle with the rest of the sunflower seeds.

38. Fermented Pumpkin Vegetables

Ingredients:

1 little pumpkin

Spices of your decision, for instance, B. mustard seeds and curry

1-2 tablespoons of salt

Directions:

Cut the pumpkin into the tiniest potential cuts or pieces.

Mix the cut pumpkin with salt and flavors.

Stir the blend appropriately, applying some weight until fluid departures. On the off chance that it doesn't, include some spring water. Now the vegetables including the next brackish water are layered in an inventive pot. Continuously leave some space within the compartment and do not top it off to the highest. Spread the vegetables with a plate, which you likewise burden. This assists with crushing out the overabundance air.

Set the container aside for seven days at temperature. You'll likewise stand by longer and strengthen the taste.

Your tolerance has paid off, you'd now be ready to eat your first self-aged vegetables.

39. Tomato Cream of Red Lentils
Fixing

¾ cup dry red lentils

1-2 canned tomatoes plate (in season 2-4 cups of cut new)

1 white onion

1 clove of garlic

1 huge carrot

1 tablespoon oil rapeseed

1-2 tablespoons of juice of a lemon

1 - 2 teaspoon cumin

1 teaspoon smoked pepper (ideally intense)

1 teaspoon appetizing or lovage

Teaspoon thyme

Decoction vegetable or water

Salt, pepper

To serve: buckwheat, parsley, coriander

Arrangement Steps

During a thick-bottomed pot or profound pan, heat the oil and fry the finely cleaved onion, at that point include garlic.

Then include the diced carrot and thus the washed lentils and pour the vegetable stock with the goal that it completely covers all Ingredients: to the tallness of 2-3 cm. Cook until carrots and lentils are delicate.

When the vegetables mellow, include canned tomatoes and flavors. Bubble for a further 10-15 minutes, at that point mix with a hand blender, add lemon squeeze, and season to taste. Present with buckwheat and new herbs.

CHAPTER 14:

JUICES AND SMOOTHIES

40.   Matcha Green Smoothie

Ingredients:

One large ripe mango (fresh or frozen)

One frozen banana

Two cups spinach

Two tbsps. Tea powder (matcha)

Half cup unsweetened almond milk

One tsp. honey

One cup of almonds (chopped)

Half cup yogurt (Greek)

Method:

Start by adding all the ingredients to a blender. Blend for one minute until the mixture turns frothy and smooth.

If you would like the smoothie a touch thick, you'll add ice cubes.

For reducing the consistency, add almond milk and blend again.

Divide the smoothie in glasses and serve chilled.

41. Tropical Kale juice

Ingredients:

One few fresh kale

One large orange

Eight carrots

One medium-sized apple

Three rounds of pineapple (one-inch)

Method:

Start by washing the ingredients and dry them.

Cut the ingredients within the proper size for accommodating them within the juicer.

Juice all the ingredients properly by employing a juicer.

You'll got to mix the juice with the assistance of a spoon in order that all the flavors can get mixed.

Divide the juice into three glasses and serve.

42.   Orange and Celery Juice

Ingredients:

Four large sticks of celery (chopped)

800 ml of fruit juice (fresh)

Five large carrots (cubed and peeled)

For garnishing

Leaves of celery

Two celery sticks (halved, peeled)

Method:

Add carrots, fruit juice, and celery to a blender. Blend all the ingredients properly until frothy and smooth.

You'll got to check the consistency of the juice and keep it up adding fruit juice consistent with your required consistency.

Blend the juice another time.

Let the juice sit within the blender for a few time.

Pour the juice into tall glasses and serve with celery sticks and leaves from the highest.

43. Kale Blackcurrant Smoothie
Ingredients:

Three tbsps. Of each

Honey or the other sweetener

Wheatgrass

One medium avocado (peeled and chopped)

One few kale (lightly steamed)

Two cups of ice cubes

Five hundred ml of coconut milk (fresh)

Two hundred grams blackcurrant (fresh or thawed)

One green apple (cored, chopped)

Method:

Start by taking a blender and add in avocado, kale, apple, coconut milk, and blackcurrant thereto. Blend the mixture until smooth.

Add honey to the mixture.

Add ice cubes to the blender and whizz the mixture once more.

Pour the smoothie in smoothie glasses.

Serve immediately and garnish with green apple at the highest.

Dust wheatgrass consistent with your need.

CHAPTER 15:

DESSERT

44.   Apple And Pear Jam With Tarragon

Preparation time: 15 minutes

Cooking time: 0 minutes

Servings: 3

Ingredients:

500g juicy pears 500g sour apples 1 large lemon

2 sprigs of tarragon 500g jam sugar 2: 1

Directions:

Peel and quarter apples and pears, remove the core and dice or grate very, very finely.

Squeeze the lemon and add to the fruit with the gelling sugar. Let the juice soak overnight!

Wash and dry the tarragon. Finely chop the leaves and add to the fruit mix.

Nutrition:

Calories: 242 Net carbs: 15g Fat: 20.5g Fiber: 3.2g Protein: 2g

45. Apple Jam With Honey And Cinnamon

Preparation time: 10 minutes

Cooking time: 15 minutes

Servings: 2

Ingredients:

300g apples 6 lemon juice

2 sticks of cinnamon 50 g liquid honey, 500g jam sugar 2: 1

Directions:

Peel and quarter the apples and remove the core.

Weigh 1 kg of pulp. Dice this finely and drizzle with lemon juice.

Mix the pulp, gelling sugar and cinnamon sticks well in a large saucepan.

After cooking remove the cinnamon sticks and stir in the honey.

Nutrition:

Calories: 193 Net carbs: 38g Fat: 4.5g Fiber: 1.8g Protein: 1.8g

46.   lum Chutney

Preparation time: 5 minutes

Cooking time: 50 minutes

Servings: 4

Ingredients:

500 g pitted prunes 50 g ginger

350 g onions

2 s vegetable oil 250g brown sugar

300ml balsamic vinegar Salt, pepper

Directions:

Quarter the washed and pitted plums. Finely dice the ginger and onions and braise in 2 s of oil. Add the plums and steam briefly.

Add the brown sugar and let it melt while stirring. Then pour balsamic vinegar over it and let it boil for about 40 minutes on a low flame.

Season with salt and pepper and pour into boiled glasses.

Nutrition:

Calories: 125 Net carbs: 19.6g Fat: 4.9g Fiber: 0.8g Protein: 1.7g

CHAPTER 16:

DESSERT RECIPES

47. Bounty Bars

Preparation Time: 10 minutes

Cooking Time: 35 minutes

Servings: 4

Ingredients:

2 cups desiccated coconut 3 coconut oil - melted

1 cup of coconut cream - full fat

4 of raw honey

1 tsp ground vanilla bean

Coating:

Pinch of sea salt

½ cup cacao powder 2 raw honey

1/3 cup of coconut oil (melted)

Directions:

Mix coconut oil, coconut cream, and honey, vanilla and salt. Pour over desiccated coconut and mix well.

Mold coconut mixture into balls and freeze. Or pour the whole mixture into a tray, freeze and cut into small bars when frozen.

Prepare the coating by mixing salt, cocoa powder, honey and coconut oil. Dip frozen coconut balls/bars into the chocolate coating, put on a tray and freeze again.

Nutrition Facts:

Calories: 120 Fat: 4.3g Carbohydrates: 16.7g Protein: 1g

48. Chocolate Cream

Preparation Time: 10 minutes

Cooking Time: 35 minutes

Servings: 4

Ingredie ts:

1 avocado

2 coconut oil

2 raw honey

2 cacao powder

1 tsp ground vanilla bean Pinch of salt

¼ cup almond milk

¼ cup goji berries

Directions:

Blend all the ingredients in the food processor until smooth and thick. Distribute in four cups, decorate with goji berries and put the fridge overnight.

Nutrition Facts:

Calories: 200kcal Fat: 4.3g Carbohydrate: 25.2g Protein: 12.8g

49.   Peanut Butter Truffles

Preparation Time: 10 minutes

Cooking Time: 30 minutes

Servings: 4

Ingredients:

5 tbsp peanut butter 1 tbsp coconut oil

1 tbsp raw honey

1 tsp ground vanilla bean

¾ cup almond flour

Coating:

Pinch of salt 1 cocoa butter

½ cup 70% chocolate

Directions:

Mix peanut butter, c all ingredients in a dough. Roll the dough into 1-inch balls, place them on parchment paper and refrigerate for half an hour (yield about 12 truffles). Melted chocolate and cocoa butter, add a pinch of salt. Dip each truffle in the melted chocolate, one at the time. Place them back on the pan with parchment paper and put in the fridge.

Nutrition Facts:

Calories: 194 Fat: 8g Carbohydrate: 13.1g Protein: 4

50.   Chocolate Pie

Preparation Time: 10 minutes

Cooking Time: 30 minutes

Servings: 4

Ingredients:

2 cups flour

1 cup dates, soaked and drained 1 cup dried apricots, chopped 1½ tsp ground vanilla bean

2 eggs

1 banana, mashed

5 cocoa powder

3 raw honey

1 ripe avocado, mashed

2 tbsp. organic coconut oil

½ cup almond milk

Directions:

In a bowl, add flour, apricots and dates finely chopped and mix. Add the banana and the eggs lightly beaten and mix.

Add vanilla, cocoa, honey, avocado and coconut oil and mix.

Add almond milk bit by bit. You could need less than ½ cup to get the right "cake consistency".

Put in a greased baking tin and cook for 30-35 minutes at 350° F. Always check the cake and allow a few more minutes if it's not done. Allow to cool before serving.

Nutrition Facts:

Calories: 380kcal Fat: 18.4g Carbohydrate: 50.2g Protein: 7.2g

CPSIA information can be obtained
at www.ICGtesting.com
Printed in the USA
LVHW080533280521
688664LV00007B/760

9 781801 863797